WORKING VOCABULARY

OTHER BOOKS BY SID GOLD

The Year of the Dog Throwers, Broadkill River Press, 2010;
Good With Oranges, Broadkill River Press. 2015;
Crooked Speech, Pond Road Press, 2018.

AWARDS

First Prize, California Poetry Society's Annual Contest, 1986, for
"Hebrew Home for the Aged"

WORKING VOCABULARY

by Sid Gold

Washington Writers' Publishing House
Washington, D.C.

for my mother and father

Grateful acknowledgment is made to the following publications in which some of these poems first appeared: *Another Small Magazine*: "From Here to L.A."; *Buckle: A Poetry Journal*: "First Bones," "Pennies," "The Supplicants"; *CQ (California Poetry Quarterly)*: "Hebrew Home for the Aged," "Some Evenings"; *Caprice*: "Last Rites"; *Cimmarron Review*: "Berry Takes Rye in December"; *Hayotzer: The Jewish-American Writer*: "Day of Atonement"; *Hungry As We Are: An Anthology of Washington Area Poets*: "Nice," "Valentine"; *The Mill*: "Mojave"; *The New Arts Review*: "Berry Works Nightwatch," "Edmund Wilson on Corbiere," "Hekyll & Jekyll," "Pasadena"; *The Prose Poem: An International Journal*: "There"; *Puerto Del Sol*: "Dad," "Karla's Snowy Song"; *The Shattered Wig Review*: "DWI," "Tenor Madness"; *Southern Poetry Review*: "Silver Bullets"; *Tar River Poetry*: "Jefferson Street"; *WordWrights*: "The Old Neighborhood."

Publication of this book is possible thanks to donations from the many Friends of Washington Writers' Publishing House.

Cover photograph by Bill Lyons
Cover design by Lynn Springer /DL Graphics Studio

ISBN 978-1-941551-27-1

Library of Congress Cataloging-in-Publication Data

Names: Gold, Sid, author.
Title: Working vocabulary / by Sid Gold.
Description: Second edition. | Washington, D.C. : Washington Writers'
  Publishing House, [2021] | Summary: "The range of this collection is
  immense; from narrative and portrait to introspective lyric, these poems
  feel as relevant today as they did at the time of their original
  publication. Gold's voice, full of the subtle wit and wry humor of the
  streets, makes readers feel as if someone is just pulling up a barstool
  and saying over a tall cold one, let me tell you a story. These poems
  see clearly and speak the honest language of everyday. Their distinctive
  energy derives from Gold's gutsy approach and from his surprising and
  delighting images. Gold's poems have the dual good sense of lacking
  pretension and of carrying evocative pictures of the life energy in his
  city of Working Vocabulary"— Provided by publisher.
Identifiers: LCCN 2021037011 | ISBN 9781941551271 (paperback)
Subjects: LCGFT: Poetry.
Classification: LCC PS3557.O3526 W67 2021 | DDC 811/.54—dc23
LC record available at https://lccn.loc.gov/2021037011

WASHINGTON WRITERS' PUBLISHING HOUSE 2814 5th Street, NE, #1301 Washington, D.C. 20017

CONTENTS

III. HONEST BARGAINERS

FOREWORD

I AM DELIGHTED that Washington Writer's Publishing House is able to offer this reissue of Sid Gold's *Working Vocabulary*, originally published in 1997 as the winner of the WWPH Poetry Prize. The range of this collection is immense; from narrative and portrait to introspective lyric, these poems feel as relevant today as they did at the time of their publication. Gold's voice, full of the subtle wit and wry humor of the streets, makes readers feel as if someone is just pulling up a barstool and saying over a tall cold one, *let me tell you a story*. But though they may convey the delightful ease and surprise of improvisations, each is a carefully crafted work of art that readers will want to return to again and again.

Gold is a master of the portrait, from Esther in "Jefferson St" who is "sentry to paperboy, postman,/ slumbering winos, woman of a thousand spasms/ & tics" to Sonny Blake in "The Yard" who works the automatic shears and steps aside to explain "over the clatter like a mortar shell,/ *It's dangerous, see, Capital D*." The speaker of these poems listens attentively to the stories his characters want to tell, respecting their need to be heard, then expands his retelling to address the audience and himself. In "Arms and the Woman," for instance, after we hear "the toughest & nastiest waitress in town" brag about her skill with "handguns & knives," the speaker turns the tables in the last lines when he says, "whatever weapons I may possess, I keep them out of sight," reminding us that the casual surface of his poems conceals a sting underneath, a stab of revelation. As Sonny Blake warns us, these poems are dangerous with a "*Capital D*," slicing through scenes of life and human behavior with such accuracy and precision that they make us catch our breath and rethink the truths we thought we knew.

The imagination is vividly present on these pages, but grounded in a healthy dose of realism. In "Last Rites," for instance, the speaker claims "my patron is a saint/ with no name, from a village/ found on no map, in a valley/ no pilgrim can reach," reminding us to be wary of any promises of revelation while at the same time offering powerful insights into human need and behavior beyond the dominion of any one religion. In "Thin Air," we are presented with a possibility— "You never know—/ as you step off the edge/ you may take flight"—but are admonished to keep this possibility to ourselves lest we grow aware of what we "stand to lose." Gold's stories and meditations are built on everyday occurrences, on the cynicism of the city and its inhabitants presented in such compelling ways that we cannot look away from their universal human truths about loneliness, labor, the need for companionship and empathy, the longing to be heard and understood, and the desire for respect. They give meaning to what we have witnessed and help us know our lives serve some purpose beyond the immediate present. They teach us "the working vocabulary/ of the blessed."

Holly Karapetkova
Vice-President, WWPH
October, 2021

I

SQUARE BUSINESS

THE YARD
for Steve Freeman

No working man could resist
the offer of a $50 tip, hard cash,
regular each Friday, but if you asked
any swinging dick in the yard
how he really felt, square business,
about working the automatic shears,
its servo-driven blades scissoring
layers of metal in a blink,
he might have told you, *sotto voce,*
avoiding your eyes, that it scared him.
And why not? All you had to do
was see them in operation, slicing lengths
of brass pipe into the sorting bin
like sausages, to envision the fingers
of your right hand lopped off
at the first knuckle, your safety glove
streaked crimson as a prize orchid.
Every so often, dawdling on my rounds
back & forth between the office
& the loading dock, I'd linger a yard
or two off Sonny Blake's shoulder
& stand humbly silent in the presence
of his casual expertise, taking in
a few quick cuts like a dilettante:
and often as not, Sonny would step aside,
pivot half-around, lift his goggles,
his hoarse growl detonating
over the clatter like a mortar shell,
It's dangerous, see, Capital D
just in case I hadn't been told.

NEEDLE PARK

They called it Needle Park,
that tree-shaded, triangular patch
at 72nd where the intersection of Broadway
& Amsterdam forms a vee, but I never saw
any needles there, or anyone shooting up,
though the word was that it had been
a junkie haven for a generation or more.
Mostly I saw the benches overflowing
with the kind of people who looked like
they could use a drink until you spied
the empty pints resting in their laps.
Disheveled, morose, & chronically beat,
they squinted past the uncertain glances
of their more fortunate neighbors
as if expecting to see their own ghosts
keeping a fixed appointment with fate.
Around them, the workaday West Side honked,
shrieked & hummed like a band tuning up.
Some time later a movie was made depicting
a preppie couple's slide into addiction.
Panic in Needle Park it was called
& the poster showed two attractive kids
who should've known better but, for reasons
never made clear, didn't, on a park bench
embracing with the desperation peculiar
to besotted lovers who fear the frenzy
that binds them will evanesce like a bubble
if they dare disengage for an instant.
The scene behind the couple is bleak,
the trees barren & scabrous, the sidewalk
deserted, & at first glance they appear
enraptured by the torture of their habits
like pilgrims crawling toward a miracle.
One might say the camera has captured

4

with perfection the perfect anguish
in their eyes, the pure terror of those
who can be certain of nothing but that
the pain of the moment is certain
only to worsen in the moments to come.
All I can tell you about any of this
is that if either of those rich white kids
had ever been hanging around Needle Park,
alone or together, I didn't see them
but then again, after some time
I'd stopped looking for anyone I knew.

HEKYLL & JEKYLL

When girls fight, they squint their eyes,
duck their faces, nails looking to scratch,
go for the face & hair

so when the double-ugly Tucker sisters
cornered her in the 3rd floor john,
she thrust her arms out & above like lances

& her hands felt like onions
because she remembered what everyone knew,
that Hekyll & Jekyll wrapped their wiry braids

in Gillette blues,
& they were leering into her shocked blood
till she spread an open, messy palm

across their bloated cheeks
& pushed through the door,
down the stairs, nursed at a water fountain,

balled thick wads of tissue in her fists
& left school
for an afternoon at the movies

realizing only then in the silvered darkness
that she had stopped bleeding
& had not screamed.

JEFFERSON ST.

Esther, sentry to paperboy, postman,
slumbering winos, woman of a thousand spasms
& tics, interrupts her jittery hobble
to greet you with a genial grimace,
hitches her dress, adjusts her horn-rims,
palms her elbows, manages two words
in a choked, guttural whine,
bows you through the front door
& resumes her vigilant patrol.
You pass shyly, watchful,
wondering what visitors must think.
Mrs. Tusch, the sweeper, fresh from a foray
into back alley refuse, swings her broom
in a relentless arc until the tiles are scarred with straw.
Her pale face tensed, sketched by a spider,
she shuffles toward a dark corner
like a lame ghost at the tap of a footstep,
averts her gaze, & claims to know nothing.
Partners in the same broken dance,
their steps circumscribed by the front lawn,
its stand of stunted evergreens,
they shadow-box across the lobby
like punchdrunk boxers:
all of the memories, none of the moves.

THE VISITORS

Upstairs in 2B, Old Man Quinn,
sworn to die in a bed all bought
& paid for, lies wheezing
like a hibernating grizzly
who's lost all hope of spring,
his workingman's hands warped
& swollen into useless paws.

Shoulders hunched, heads bowed
into the wind, his relations
arrive in twos & threes,
hobble-stepping down the walk,
their jaws set like magistrates
about to hear a final plea.
Beneath their feet, dry leaves
crackle like burning logs.

In the hallway, their voices
echo off the walls like swordplay
& after they have passed,
their scent—sweaty, pungent—
remains, hanging in the stillness
like aging sides of beef.

NICE

it's nice to have
a beer
in the middle of the afternoon
say about 3:30
as if you had nothing
better
to do   nothing
to lose
thinking about all
those poor stiffs working
the loading dock who'll be
too beat after years
of it
to get stiff anymore
until they're laid out   stiff
a phony peace painted
on their mugs with rouge
thinking about maybe
what you'll do for dinner
read the paper real slow
coffee & pie
it feels
so good
dreaming about that beer that paper
while you're stacking those
damned crates & checking them
against the bill
of lading
it almost makes you
horny
if you don't watch out

LEAPING FOOL
for Merrill Leffler

To look at him, you wouldn't have thought Frank Seratovich
was a ballplayer, with his doofy thick black-rimmed glasses, big
nose, & cowlick no amount of goo could keep down, not to
mention those sleeveless guinea tee-shirts & cuffed khaki
chinos he wore. He looked more like a grocery store delivery boy
or maybe a local greaser-in-training than a schoolyard legend.
But despite his un-hip appearance, Seratovich could jump
right out of the sky. Standing only about 6, 6-one, at sixteen
he had the shoulders & neck of a prizefighter. Using his
strength to screen you off, he could set up under the basket, call
for the ball, & power up & out toward the rim, carrying you
on his back, his hands clamped around the ball like a vise, his
elbows akimbo. If you weren't careful, you might lose a few
teeth to an elbow or crack your jaw on a shoulder if you leaned
in too close. Drifting out on a wing, he could take a pass on
the weak side & get through the traffic in the paint in two
dribbles, skying toward the hoop as if he had tiny jets in his heels.
If you got tired or lazy, letting him roam in the lane & forgetting
to put a hand on him, he might just throw it down over you. Not
bad for a white boy, everybody agreed: a genuine leaping fool.
He was also, by the time he hit eighteen, a stone junkie. Al-
ways a bit out-of-control, he gave even the rough-&-tumble
Christian Brothers at Rice more than they could tolerate, bud-
ding hoop star or not, but now things got serious. Somewhere
along the line he'd picked up a habit & soon it was only a
matter of time till he started getting nabbed for all manner of
burglaries, not to mention the possession raps. By the time I
got to meet Frank face-to-face, he must have been over 25 &
had already done two or three, so to speak, light stretches. Down
at the park, out on parole & determined, he swore, to stay clean,
he lingered near the benches just outside the playground fence,

10

his back to the basketball court, & gave us the rundown on life on the inside while occasionally glancing over his shoulder at an ongoing game like a man distracted now & again by an unexpected noise. He had made some of the usual stops on the circuit—Dannemora, Matteawan, Fishkill, Coxsackie—& although his tales held no surprises—when to turn your back & when not, who to trust & who not, who bent over easily & who didn't—he delivered them with a medium-pitched, unassuming emphasis that told you to pay attention. And after a while he would edge closer to the fence, his arms folded, watching the game in silence with the mournful but resigned eyes of a peregrine who, no longer deemed trust-worthy by his handlers, had had his wings permanently clipped.

THE OLD NEIGHBORHOOD

I knew a lot of people
when I was a kid
& not one of them is famous.

We'd hang out together,
not doing much, really, except
bum cigarettes & say stuff like
Man, you ain't nothing.
Ain't never gonna be nothing.

Now when we run into each other,
we keep our distance,
give one another a long, hard look
or a quick nod.

Each of us wishes he could be
the first to say *What did I tell you*
& no one smokes anymore.

DUKE'S PLACE

I once stood in Chang's Finest Hand Laundry at 74th & Amsterdam & watched as a local numbers boss named Duke, a beefy, wide-shouldered hard-ass with the precise pompadour & mustache of a dandy past his prime, chiseled down a junkie from his asking price of $20 to $15 for a hot leather coat. The junkie was this tall, skeletal, fair-haired cat about 30 who hung out at the pool hall above the Five & Dime on 79th when times were flush, cracking wise with the regulars at the one-pocket tables & making side-bets he never paid, but now, trying as he might to be cool, he was sweating coldly & seemed afflicted by an irregular series of twitches & tics while his eyes glowed with the nervy despair of those who, although quite ill, fear the cure more than the disease. A moment earlier he'd entered the shop, a dim, narrow room, unfurnished but for a front counter & long rows of shelves disappearing into a dark, indefinite rear, & offered the coat to Duke or either of the hangers-on standing at Duke's side, all the while swearing it was fresh, taken only moments ago from a Mark IV parked on 61st & worth $200 at the least. Indeed, the coat was a prize, knee-length & double breasted, its soft, honey-brown leather at once both firm & pliant to the touch, but Duke, holding the garment by its collar, merely gave it a glance, announced his price, & shrugged. Try this man here, Duke said, meaning me, silent throughout. At the time, I had some knowledge of the cruelty certain men inflict upon others, but I had as yet not learned it by heart. I looked to Chang, just then resting his arms on the counter, his rheumy, heavy-lidded eyes mute & immutable behind a veil of cigarette smoke, but he did nothing but finger my packet of starched button-downs, nudging it an inch or two toward me before he turned & ducked noiselessly back into the shadows. Coat won't fit me, I began, but Duke would have none of it, cutting off my halting excuses with a sharp, derisive snort as his brace of flunkies, thickset men with the rapacious stares of born preda-tors, chortled at my discomfort like lusting swine. They couldn't have cared less what I had to say, or what I thought, or even that I had been standing there all along, watching.

RAZOR BLADES

Years ago, a friend,
then 20 & in the service,
watched a young prostitute armed
with slivers of razor blades
taped between her fingers slash
the face of a graying hustler
threatening to slap her silly
on the pavement outside a strip
of sleazy joints opposite
the taxi stand where my friend,
anxiously eyeing the time,
stood waiting for his buddies.
Just a moment earlier, the hustler,
all shark-skin & sharp-creases,
had followed the prostitute out
one of the bars onto the sidewalk
grabbing after her & shouting
You Bitch! You Cheap Bitch!
but now blood streamed down
his cheeks like flaming tears
as he reeled, howling, his face
in his palms, staggering back
on his heels like a boxer covering up.
My friend told me this story years
after the event, over a beer,
away from the wife, by that time
feeling maybe just a bit unsettled
by his seeming respectability
& longing to recapture the rawness
of his response to events both lurid
& off-beat, and I, ever mindful
of protocol, responded to it
with the bright silence appropriate
for the youth who finds himself

among those more worldly than he.
But what of the two antagonists?
What became of our battlers, parting
as they did, to pursue separate fates?
Did the bested grifter, his wounds
stanched with tissue, lurch
into the john of a busy pool hall,
gaze into the mirror & divine
at once his destiny, his lot?
Did he envision a face certain
to serve as an indelible reminder
of a whore's violent disrespect?
Examining the acute slashes,
did he, wide-eyed, fancy the prospect
of a pattern of chevrons not unlike
the scarring incised in rituals
marking a boy's initiation as a man?
Did he, exhausted, his doctoring
completed, sneak into a storeroom
& seek his rest upon a daybed?
And once there, did he dream
of another country, a far-off land
in which hateful wenches receive
their just rewards & old men
are treated with due respect.
Did he arise restored, his blood
stinging with vinegar & spit,
& vowing revenge, remove a pistol
received as payment for a debt
from the bottom of a footlocker,
fingering it like a talisman?
Or did he do nothing of the kind,
deciding instead he was quits
once & for all, with short cons

& fat marks, with motel rooms let
by the week, with business cards
& licenses stolen from the dead?
Did the hooker, gathering herself,
flee into the nearest alleyway
furiously insisting *That Scumbag,*
I Should Have Cut His Throat
& promising her pimp would send
some guys expert at breaking legs?
Did she unball her fist, & opening
her palm, find a man's dark blood
where she'd hoped to see a lifeline?
Did she look into that red stain
& remember the eyes of her victim
as the blades sliced his cheeks?
Did two small children, a girl
& a boy, seeing her in that alley
walk uncertainly up to her & ask,
the way small children do, *Lady*
are you okay? Are you all right?
At a loss for an answer, did she
reach down, take the girl's wrist
between her thumb & forefinger
& with her thumb gently trace
the path of a vein blue as ink?
Or did she, suddenly calculating
& resolute, score so much dope
that she could be confident
of losing most of an entire week
in a narcotic mist, counting on
the routine of johns & fixes
to fog her memory forever?
For better or worse, a calculus
capable of plotting the points

of the arcs upon which these lives
are poised is far beyond our ken
& accuracy demands we confine
our claims to what is clearly known.
Two people met in a confrontation
worthy of notice for the nature
of its violence & combatants
while a third, at some distance,
did nothing other than record
the event on his memory's film
with such exactitude that time
& time again he would summon it
for display on the silver screen
of his discourse upon demand,
satisfied that through its telling
his audience would accept it
as truth & as such a body
of facts complete & sufficient
in itself, just as I have told
you, just as I, myself, was told.

BERRY TAKES RYE IN DECEMBER

From my high stool
I can watch the bitter wind
twist small, crisp piles of leaves
into flame.
Catty-corner across Crescent
two men leave a pine-board windowed deli

& lift cases of beer
into an idling station wagon.
They stamp once or twice,
blow into the muzzle of their cupped hands,
begin a closed-lip smile.

The bartender hovers nearby,
a benign tout in his brown plaid sportscoat.
I silently name him *Stash*.
He calls me *sir*,
pours my neat rye smooth,

returns to his Slovak argument
among pea-coats at the far end.
The voices are raised, direct enough
for soccer or landlords.
New words bounce & spread
like hot coffee emptied in one gulp.
No one grins: it is not about women.

WHAT HE TOLD ME

I never saw Saigon

We'd come into a clearing, the air still as fresh snow
there'd be a grunt from some patrol hung up in a tree
with his dick cut off, stuck in his mouth like a cigar

The acka-acka on top of you & all around divots tore up
from the strafing, everybody scattering like cockroaches
in heat, so I dove for a crater no bigger than a pothole
you wouldn't have lost a dog in there, headfirst, knees
tucked against my stomach like a foetus in a mason jar
squirreled myself in so tight when it was over they had
to tug me out like a stump before I suffocated

This scar here?

Didn't notice I was hit until I reached down to wipe
the sweat & come up red-handed. Fought all through
the night feeling numb as dry ice on that side
By then shock had set in

When did it wear off?
Ain't wore off since marijuana been invented

North of Da Nang

HURT DANCE

Two gangs met up one night at Buddy's Billiards, a bare, over-bright basement room previously believed to be neutral turf. The Woodside bunch had a clear purpose in mind, so in moments cue sticks were slicing the air like machetes & if you happened to be the wrong guy caught bending over to line up a shot, you might have found your face all of a sudden mashed like a steam iron against the green felt, some creep doing a hurt dance on your skull with his fists. Bystanders played hide 'n' seek behind the corner tables, feigning invisibility as they witnessed a cruel ballet so manic you might have thought its choreographers were on something more potent than just an adrenaline high, or scatted toward the stairs leading to the street, already affecting the distracted air of skilled amnesiacs. But it was over in seconds & didn't even make much noise, not even Jackie Gennaro's parting shot: a cue ball sidearmed like a peg to first at the forehead of a crumpled Bobby Flynn from five feet away as Jackie spun to eyeball the room, making sure all his guys were out. You could say it was almost an afterthought, really.

KARLO'S SNOWY SONG

February & as I chip & stab
a frozen evening's snowfall from my windshield
Pap Pennington & his grandson, Karlo,
stalled forever at some point between toddler
& pre-teen, come through the alleyway.
Shod in galoshes, wearing earmuffs,
rain-resistant hunter's caps,

they nod 20° in my direction,
venture a blinking, diffident smile
that does not quite bare teeth,
slide their wool-gloved hands
into deep overcoat pockets & scuff a path
past the line of avalanched cars.

Pap, his skin like iced vellum,
has not aged since my memory, & Karlo,
stocky, indeterminate, his walk broad-shouldered
& stolid, is ageless, though now
the gun-metal shadow of shaved stubble
covers his jaw. I watch them step
onto son & father Pal's open, faded porch
& as Pap stamps through the screened doorway

Karlo remains, spreading & closing his arms
across his chest, noiselessly clapping
while singing, like a trombone glissing down a well,
his strident, hoarse song to mid-winter,
the likes of which most men have never heard.

NORTHEAST SALVAGE

Partner in the oldest yard in town,
Morrie welcomes my boss's arrival
with the wry half-grin & feigned shock
reserved for brothers in the trade,
gives me, a newcomer, the once-over
in a glance, nods once at hearing my name.
This is platinum, he confides, winking,
a lounge act setting up his punchline,
& fingering a broach-sized thingamajig
plucked at random from the several
on his desk, he disassembles its innards
with the deft, patient sleight-of-hand
of a card-sharp until he extracts a coil
of vermicelli-gauge wires easily mistaken
for gold if only gold had somehow had
its color washed from it & left behind
a pale, silverish metal that inhaled
the faint, dying breath of gold
from the surrounding available light.
Watch me, he intones, twisting & bending
each strand back & forth, up & down
in a demonstration of its mettle.
Only platinum does this, he counsels.
Everything else, even gold, will break.
The lesson over, he settles back, waves
at two pails off to the side chock full
of components like the one he holds.
Those two buckets, each one, 15,000.
For the first time I begin taking stock
of the room where Morrie makes his office,
its half-lit confines so cluttered
with angular bulk that it's difficult

to distinguish the shadowy from the real.
Two grated windows placed high above
eye level enable a soft, bleached light
to brighten a cranny or two with a color
difficult to place or name: platinum.

PENNIES

One summer I was a bit short.

I emptied the dark vase
across the kitchen table,
turning it mouth down
with the deliberate arc
of my elbow raised
& rolled twenty-two wrappers
of pennies in one sitting.
I watched them gather: flat, round grubs
skidding away from the steady light
of an overturned stone.
Some were a high orange.
I plucked those first,
forefinger & thumb working
like hungry men.
The scent of copper's dull grease
remains on my hands.

There is nothing new about this.
It has been done by every one of us.
The boarded entrance to the mine
frames my campfire against the night:
dry leaves & two blankets
make a fine bed.

II

A SAINT WITH NO NAME

LAST RITES

I am a member of no church
& hence it is fitting
my patron is a saint
with no name, from a village
found on no map, in a valley
no pilgrim can reach.
His relics, about which
tradition is vague, vanished
long ago, lost with those folios
of his *Meditations* not stolen
by thieves on the road to Rome,
& the two faded likenesses
that survive are remarkably unalike.
Despite his suspect hagiography,
I remain undiscouraged, tethered
to my faith like a guard dog
for no singular reason save that
when I am alone, I feel no presence
other than his, hear no voice
other than his whisper
counseling me, urging me
to do nothing, often, in his name.

THE CHOICE

Would I, given a second chance,
begin once again at the beginning.
Would I, nearsighted as a mole,
push toward the light, having learned
that the human heart waxes & wanes
like a capricious moon,
some days open as the hand
that shares, other days closed
like a fist, that on dark mornings
that refuse to be named I will awaken
with the taste of the ashes
of other men's bones in my mouth
& at night as I lay down I will search
the sky, wondering why not one
blinking star fulfilled its promise &,
finding no other answer, blame myself.
Would I start all over knowing
that 1949 will be remembered only
as one more year that had exhausted
all its miracles long ago,
that I would seek out my name
in thick ledgers only to feel
each page crumble under my fingers,
that in time I would come to find
the taste of blood & the taste
of wine to be one & the same.
And would I have any other choice
but to stand here saying this
to a people who have learned to turn
a deaf ear to good news & embrace tragedy
like a long-lost daughter, holding
in my palm a small chunk of a dead star
like a weighted die, wagering what remains
of the riven cloak of my spirit
to bring a distant sun closer to the Earth
piece by burning piece.

THIN AIR

You never know—
as you step off the edge
you may take flight,
soaring freely on the high road
above pettiness & deceit.
You may discover thin air
supports a full-grown weight
& stand in place, suddenly renewed,
or be caught, perhaps,
by a discreet angel assigned
to preserve those who dare.
Upon your return, above all
keep this incident to yourself,
explaining your reticence as a hangover,
your thoughtfulness as the flu.
Never recount this wonder,
guide others to the precipice,
offer to demonstrate the technique.
Subjected to badgering,
you will be tempted to try again.
Close-mouthed, goaded by skeptics,
you will approach the peak heavy with awe,
frayed as old cloth by self-doubt,
never more aware of what may await you
& what you stand to lose.

HEBREW HOME FOR THE AGED

Two hundred miles away lies my grandmother
like a dried fig, lungs rotting into brackish foam.
Weekends I Metroliner northward
& sit listening to her puzzle together
the fragments of a shaman's prayers,
half-forgotten lyrics of another lifetime,
another tribe.

It is for you, kinde, that I pray,
groans this Litvak seamstress,
eternally dyspeptic & forever on the lookout
for a bargain with either Lord or Dybbuk,
seventy-two years removed from Djahvehnashuk,
its streets overrun with caftans, ox-carts
& mud, the anarchist cells of Vilna.
Hide the pamphlets in pots hung on the wall,
she cautions me, a crafty gleam set momentarily aflame
in the shallow oil slick of her eye
by memory's elusive spark.
As she speaks, her mottled hand clings to my forearm
like a scab.

On the dresser I uncover a cropped photograph
of her brother, Eli, the one with one small toe
too many, and a friend.
Both in their twenties, they look for all the world,
in their embroidered, belted tunics,
as though they had been cast for Karamazov.

Eli, one angled elbow propped
on his companion's shoulder like a spar,
has my grandmother's brooding eyes
& the poker-faced gaze of those resigned
to a universe composed of riddles
that will not solve.

Eli's friend, smooth black waves sleeked back
from his forehead like an otter, has a bristling mustache
& the amiably-confident, sharp-eyed glance
of the picaro measuring his mark.
He holds a pipe & resembles a youthful Joe Stalin.
No one can remember his name, or the occasion.

AND MILES TO GO
for Paul Wingo

That evening
I first heard Miles, saw Miles
at the skating rink in Central Park
I sat in the dollar bleachers
50 yards, give or take, from the stage
all of eighteen & ready to believe.
When they introduced Miles, I squinted
toward the cone of polished space
encircling him & said to myself
That's Miles! He's my man!
During each number I watched him
step away from the Quintet's loose weave,
that famed question-mark stance
punctuating the night, & stand a yard
or two off by himself like a man
so accustomed to the gaze of others
he wore their stares as casually as a second skin,
heard Miles take his own bittersweet time
with each phrase no matter how fast
or slow the tempo as if trying to recall
the melody's blue dream of itself,
some notes a stiletto piercing
the heart of a ghost, some notes
a gleaming blade cutting through fog,
others that same blade spreading
sometimes butter, sometimes jam
& each solo offering an answer
to a question you didn't know you'd asked.
There are times someone will mention
Miles in passing or I'll hear
something of his on the car radio

or under the din of conversation in a bar.
My man's gone now, I'll say to myself
in a murmur reserved for secrets
or prayer, although for the life of me
I can't remember the tune.

MOJAVE

In the California desert
names are of other places,
brisk & bittersweet:
Essex, Baghdad, Cadiz.
No one dare make this place
his own.

Outside Needles a teenage boy,
mustachioed faint as frost,
jig-steps along the westbound blacktop.
His hand-lettered sign names a city
everyone has visited, lived in, or left.
Hordes of cacti sentry the open desert,
men caught wearing silly hats
& planted as a reminder:
green shadows of towns.

The boy brushes the woolen wind
from his salt-rimmed eyes,
thinks of lizards sluggish
till sundown, the number of days
a rattler takes to shed
its paper-dry, used-up skin.

DAY OF ATONEMENT

Yorn Kippur, the brick steps
of my grandfather's porch
& I sit squeezing
a *spaldeen* out of round,
my high-topped sneakers
dry-docked like small boats,
my father beside me in chinos
grabbing an irreverent smoke
while clans of the Orthodox
garbed in proper Ghetto black,
observant down to the canvas
covering their feet, file past
on the journey toward repentance,
their ear-locks swaying
in the chant-time measure
of each rubber-soled step.
No leather today, my father explains
between puffs, it's a rule.

Eyes lowered as if in prayer,
I begin tightening the laces of my Keds.

THE BLESSED

Sometimes
I am caught unawares

Nothing, no one, around me
seems guarded or frightened
& I need not strike out
out of vanity or fear

I confess:
these moments are so unexpected
I am somewhat at a loss,
unaccustomed to a life unhampered
by the need to explain

I am learning at such times
to say nothing,
to accept such occasions
with a restful but alert silence

the working vocabulary
of the blessed

INTIMACY

In every heart there can be found
a chamber in which intimacy,
a pure spirit much like the essence
of a flame, is thought to reside.
An exact knowledge of the workings
of this vessel still defies
the best efforts of medical science,
but it is known that blood circulates
through these alien precincts rarely,
if ever, in a lifetime, for if it does,
one's blood thickens like impasto
& the heart swells dangerously,
deepening in color like a bruise.
Alone, the stricken sit motionless,
reciting snatches of past conversations
in a murmur punctuated by sighs,
watching with inordinate interest
as the day's faithful shadow
splays its shroud across the wall.
What spell is this? they may demand
in a fervid whisper. *What conjury*
possesses the power to penetrate
the heart without piercing the flesh?

TENOR MADNESS

At 3 A.M.
John Coltrane
his liver flaking with rust
his eyes heavy-lidded & rapt
sits on the curb
outside the Stop 'N' Shop, waiting
for an uptown bus, dreaming the music
of a lost dynasty

Months now, every impulse
had become a furious riff of honks
& squeals, gruff grizzly groans
cascades of double-tongued bleats & trills
whispery bellows like breaths
of dry ice, screeches carving the night like a jigsaw
belly-bent sixteenth notes blowing deserts
into bloom
harmonies for songs heard only
by the bone choir of his inner ear

Just over the glare of the spotlight
was a blank space
thick with enemies, their eyes shards
of mirrors, their voices sputtering rage
like a tailpipe, demons
who swallowed every note & vomited bats
hungering for the blood money of his soul

And Coltrane
blood jangling like loose change
would leave the stand, hang at the corner
one ear curled toward the soft tickle of laughter
from passing cars, a trio of charwomen
staring at him like maiden aunts at church
starved cowfrogs prophesying

ages of plague
& the youngblood rent-a-cop, silent
behind his tin star & Papa Doc shades
Mr. Streetwise hisbadself
who never betrayed surprise
not even when a shaved sliver of glissando
snapped out the bell of Trane's tenor
& stung—no, sung—October's last surviving blue bottle
back back back
into the ghost of a prayer
for you

BERRYWORKS NIGHTWATCH

The secret is hear nothing

and everything.
Last night I heard lions roar.
The night before, wolves.

Any evening I expect to hear the buzzer,
walk to the door & find a tiger kitten,
a wispy pouch of spindly golden bones,
eyes unopened, tucked in swaddling clothes
with a scrawled note: Stolen from its litter—
do your best.

In a few years
I'll be stalking this wing on all fours,
able to catch the scent of fear

at 600 yards.

FIRST BONES

If I cannot sleep

during the night,
I listen

for the rhythm of my first bones:
tiny men,

grown whole from beads of light,
singing the thick, fur-laden notes

of dense ferns
that sprout

in the oily forest loam,
roots nourished

by the blood of deer
startled as they bend

their soft ears toward the wind.
Their cloven hooves

sink steadily into the earth
as my desperate men beneath

pull mightily
for their own lives' sake.

SOME EVENINGS

Some evenings we could all,
each one of us, run headlong
to the nearest cliff,
its wooden restraining barriers
long reduced to kindling
by those seeking an alternative,
artists of a canvas too broad
for a single heart to frame,
& wonder if becoming air-borne
were more a state of mind
or condition of the spirit
than anything else,
a dream too flammable, *we think*,
for this ignescent night:
it drifts like smoke
from our outstretched arms
into an embrace of ghosts,
a dream's own bridge across a chasm,
while all around us night burns
like a dark flame.

SUCKERPUNCH

The other day
I stood at the mirror
& saw some wise-ass
staring me down,
just itching for a fight.

Recognizing his type,
I lowered my glance
as if continuing on my way
& jerking my shoulder
caught him, leaning in,
right between the eyes,
shattering that superior look
into a mosaic of shards.

My luck has been improving
ever since.

DWI

What is left
when all that remains
is to pump a few bucks worth
into the tank & speed up & down
some dark, empty straightaway,
drunk with fever,
the wheel a swizzle stick
& the wind shattering like ice,
until the night is nothing more
than a tableau conjured in a dream?

Ah, Beauty,
stand astride the white line
so all the rude boys
can blow through your skirts
like bulls following a cape.
Your smile is the horizon
arcing across the sky.

SILVER BULLETS

There is always the possibility
the bullet may pass straight through,
taking your headaches with it,
giving onlookers a unique window
through which to view events.
Despite the airshaft bored
through skull & brain—in one temple,
out the other—you're unchanged
but for certain improvements:
your thoughts, so often cramped,
have room to stretch out, unwind,
& merely turning sideways into the wind
clears your head of stuffiness.
Don't fret about appearances:
the neat hole explains everything—
your walk, feet barely touching ground,
your cheshire cat grin,
your lack of guile & guilt, heat & blood.
The bullet itself will keep traveling,
in search of other lives in need of a quick fix.
No target is beyond its range.

THE SUPPLICANTS
for Martin Galvin

It is noon.
The old women kneel at prayer,
their prayerbooks yellowed
like uncut fingernails.

We, the faithless,
trade jibes and tear
at thick-crusted bread
while each single-braid
sways in chant-time rite.
One shale-face lifts
her blade of chin,
a reaching into time's basket
of reeds: the sun bobs
on a white-hot string.
The landlord refills
his carved pipe, tamps it
for an even burn, & turns
with a closed-mouth smile
toward his fields.
In the orchard locusts,
hungry, winged whetstones,
begin their dry shudders.
This morning the brewery wagon
emptied at the barn door.

Now our breath stands quiet:
the teams of tuft-legged dray horses
lower their heads
into wooden water troughs.

Later, the curled odor of damp beans.

III

HONEST BARGAINERS

VALENTINE

I told you
I had nothing to offer
beyond what you could see
but you didn't pay me any mind
& the next morning you're already up,
quiet as a shoplifter,
regarding my prints
like accusers caught in lies,
eyeing my closets as if severed limbs
were concealed in the shelves,
your ear cocked, tapping the walls
for hidden safes, secret passageways,
whatever it is a woman can determine
from sounds a man stops noticing
the first time his woman moves on.
While I shaved, you stepped
out of your jeans & curled
your thigh into mine, pressed
your lips just beneath my ear,
& watched fresh blood streak my jaw
like warpaint before whispering
our late breakfast could wait later still.
It is too soon for pet names
so we'll hold our tongues,
but when you straddle down over me,
the sweat on our foreheads
beading like dew, let's sit up,
our shoulders squared, & stare
into the mirrors of each other's eyes
like honest bargainers
& see who smiles first.

DRAW ONE
for James C. L. Brown

An ex-lover tends bar
at a beer joint down the street.
Afternoons when I stop in,
she pours me a draft & leaves it,
wordlessly, at the far corner
of the bar, waves me off
when I try to hand her a bill
& lighting a smoke,
retreats to her lookout
in the doorway to the back room
where her old man is throwing darts.

I nod a quick thanks
& take a seat in an alcove
angled away from the board.
Every time he scores doubles or trebles
she lets out a short moan:
when he's in the wrong bed or goes bust,
a barely audible sigh.

Just by listening closely,
I can figure out the score.

THE GIFT

I do what I do,
live as I live,
as best I can.
Others
their good intentions
warming them like a cloak
urge me
to change.
It would give them great pleasure,
they say, to see me happy.
But I know better.
I see their pity,
the dark joys
they treasure like keepsakes,
beneath their solicitous glances
like disfiguring scars
obscured by a beard.
Such is the gift I carry with me, always.
It needs no occasion
but my arrival.

ARMS & THE WOMAN

By now the bars have closed & a dark breeze off the water is be-
ginning to cool the tail-end of a day so hot it stunned us all into
silence for fear our words would burst into flame. For an hour she
has been telling me how she's the toughest & nastiest waitress in
town, how skilled she is with handguns & knives, & I believe her,
believe everything she has said, & tell her so, nodding along with
her words like a back-beat. How back on the farm she warned
off trespassers by shooting out the radiators of their cars, how
one night she rousted a bunch of drugdealers from the breezeway
of her rowhouse with a drawn .38, how she realized both her for-
mer husbands were washouts within hours after the weddings,
how she now has several boyfriends but lets each one know exactly
where he stands, how she is sometimes taken for younger than her
daughter, how she likes to think of herself as *aggressive* but not *violent*;
all this while pausing only for breath, her eyes glittering with the
distant passion of sequins. And me? I'm dressed for the season &
glad of it, for if she cares to examine me personally, she will plainly
see that whatever weapons I may possess, I keep them out of sight.

KELSEY'S TRICK

Crowded into the crush
of a clubby singles bar
at half-past Friday night,
man-mountain Kelsey, freshly-shorn
& pumpkin-faced for the occasion,
loafs like a domesticated bear,
lazily renewing old acquaintances.

A few arrivals unbutton just inside the door
& wiping mist from their glasses
squint toward the barroom,
pathfinders mapping new terrain.
All the women must have flown South
before the rates went up, or maybe Vegas,
cashing in their chips.

Kelsey leans against the paneled wall,
one arm dangling from a coat-hook
curved like a finger beckoning
whatever angels may be hovering above.
A foaming beer mug in his off hand,
he bends the hook toward the floor,
then back, shrugs at his success,
muses *I can still do that trick*
although no one had voiced any doubts
& empties his beer in audible glugs
as if the mug itself were next.

In the street outside,
a cold-hearted wind foments an argument
with itself & wedge-nosed coupes
whine across the intersection,
headlights beaming into the bay windows
like the eyes of giant insects
searching for a nest to lay their eggs.

EDMUND WILSON ON CORBIERE

Corbiere, son of a Breton sea captain,
chose the life of an outlaw.
Full of dismal groanings & vulgar wit,
he went about in convict's clothing,
once fired a revolver from his window
at the village choir.

In Paris, he slept daylong,
spent his nights in cafes,
consumptive, writing in a fever.
Come dawn he loitered before the precinct house,
greeting the paroled harlots
with the half-tender, half-harsh outrages
of a fellow exile.

On a visit to Rome he walked the streets
wearing white-tie and a Bishop's mitre,
led a beribboned pig on a leash,
painted two eyes on his forehead.

His poetry, slangy slapdash fantasy,
self-mocking & savage, would rise
without warning, as Huysmans said,
to a cry of sharp pain like the snap
of a cello string.

THE LEAP

When Sternheim glanced down
from his rooftop perch into the street below,
he saw himself plummeting 17 floors
like a water balloon launched as a prank.
Stepping back from the railing, he stared
into the dark mirror of his spit-shined oxfords
& envisioned his stocky frame spread-eagled
in the gutter, his ribs crushed
& splintered like pretzels in a sack.

The week just past a city commissioner,
caught feeding too hungrily
at the public trough, had stepped
from a seventh floor ledge on West 86th
only to lay badly broken but still alive
on the asphalt like a maimed, overturned beetle
as he struggled to lift himself off his back
& walk away from the smear of his life.

Six floors beneath sat Sternheim's parents
like two aged marionettes:
his mother, adjusting the doilies
on the armchairs, her good ear
cocked toward the front door; his father
in a fresh white shirt, fiddling
with the radio dial, taking note of the hour.
Above, the sun throbbed like a gas jet
over the Hudson, points west.

BAR TALK

Kid,
he says,

Bucky Raye was
real lucky.

       Hit the number
maybe 20, 25 times a year

until the night he keels over
   WHAAP! just like that
getting off his stool.

Whatwashe? 50?

       Myself
I ain't real lucky. I'm 72.

My luck stinks, I tell him.

Goodforyoukid, he says.
Good for you.

DINER

We two are sitting quietly
at the counter, staring
into our second cups of joe,
nothing strange about us
except that we're strangers,
a truth quickly determined
by the sour-pussed hulk,
his face like raw steak,
hunkered in the corner
a few stools to our left.
But that's enough for him,
plastered before noon
& always keeping an eye out
for someone new to blame
for the fact of his birth.
According to our waitress,
this old boy's name is *Rip*.
32, single, & pregnant,
she's seen his act before,
doesn't even redden or pause
when he calls her a fat slut
every other minute or so.
By now the locals, fascinated
by their spoons, have bowed
their heads like mourners.
Sniffing the air like hounds,
they purse their lips, trade
knowing glances on the sly.
Rip has news for us all
but not much of it is good.
As far as he's concerned
the entire world sucks
& whoever doesn't like it
can kiss his sweet ass,

especially us, sitting off
to his right, for being
who we are, for happening by.
Now if we were schoolboys
aching to act out the deeds
imaged in our schoolboy dreams
& Rip were merely a bully
ready for the taking by those honest,
courageous, & true,
we'd be on him in an instant,
doing our best to rid the world
of another menace to the peace.
Yet for better or for worse
on this day we find ourselves
grown men & one quick look
into Rip's malevolent eyes
reveals his own dream vision
of our battered frames
slumped between the stools,
bruised & bleeding like winos
who've fallen in the street.
And so, feigning an air
of casual self-assurance,
we rise from our seats
in silence, slide a five
across the counter, & leave.
Outside the known universe
seems to sigh with relief
while we, eyes forward,
step wordlessly to the car
& slip behind the wheel,
so filled with self-loathing
we dare not speak aloud.

BROTHER DEAN

Jerry's younger brother Dean was fishing along the old canal with his girlfriend Karen around 11:00 on a Sunday night in late July. It was a hot, muggy night, the air pressing against their skins like a wet towel. As best as they could tell, they were alone. Two guys wearing baggy pleated slacks & fancy tee shirts came down the path, one behind the other. They asked Dean if he wanted any coke. No, Dean said, glancing at Karen to say nothing. Cool, said the first one, shrugging as if he expected as much. Dean watched as the two of them turned & walked back down the path toward the road, but he was not surprised when an hour later he & Karen saw them leaning against Karen's Corolla. Dean looked up & down the shoulder for another car, but he couldn't find one. Sure you don't want some coke?, the talker asked when they got within earshot. No bread, my man, Dean replied, opening the driver's side door. It all happened quickly after that. The talker flashed a knife & Dean, admitting there was a roll of bills under the floormat & appealing to them to let him & Karen just walk away afterwards, reached down under the seat where he knew he had left a ballpeen hammer for no particular reason he could think of at the time. Then he rose fast, all at once, swinging the hammer in a sort of improvised combination left-hook upper-cut motion that landed so quickly you might have missed it unless you had known it was coming. The first swing caught the talker squarely on the right temple, dropping him onto one knee, & the next two or three had him lying flat on his back, lifeless, one side of his skull bashed in like an uninflated basketball. The quiet one had taken off as soon as his buddy had fallen. You could just about make out his yellow shirt seeming to float around the next curve like a lightning bug. About 4:00 A.M. two state troopers knocked on the door of Dean's group house. Karen, too upset to sleep, had gotten jittery & called the County about what had gone down. The County, in turn, threw the case to the State, who sent the troopers, who seemed, to say the least, surprisingly unconcerned. Why'd you have to hit him more than once?, one cop at the scene asked before adding that Dean would most likely be okay. Because there was no way I could know if he couldn't still get up, Dean said without blinking. I learned about all this on Thursday when I went to see Jerry about getting my car tuned up in his driveway sometime soon. Jerry waved me into the kitchen while Dean worked on a case of Heinekens on the couch. He'd turned twenty-two just a month earlier. Leave before he gets too drunk, Jerry advised. And keep the conversation light, he cautioned me. The kid's had a rough week.

HAPPY HOUR
for Suzanne St. Onge

The fate I fear most
is standing beside me at the bar,
his face leached red with fever
& booze, smelling faintly
like a fouled sump & belching
half-audible curses into his rye.
I'm avoiding conversation & he knows it.
His rheumy eyes, unblinking as a cat's,
radiate the sullen malice of an ex-pug
who has lost his last dozen brawls
& looks forward to losing the next.

I seen you somewheres,
he swears: I fear there is
a fighting chance he's right.
Setting down his shot & wiping
his hands with the precise nonchalance
of a rummy adept at working a room
with nothing but spit & bluster,
he pivots to face me dead on,
squares his shoulders, cocks his chin,
& tells me so, gathering himself
like a counterpuncher measuring a jab.

By now our wrangling
has attracted attention.
The bartender drifts toward us
with just enough commotion
to draw my eye, tucks his forearms
beneath the counter where he's stashed
a nightstick like an old bone.
The well-fed frat boys clustered
near the window begin to edge closer,
their libidos loosed by beer

& the coy giggling of their dates,
their eyes itching with blood.
I can feel my heart settling
in the back of my mouth like a chunk
of beef, waiting to be chewed.

DAD

Past midnight he would enter his bathroom,
stay there for hours.
We used to think he was ill, or drunk,
but I peeked & saw him leaning out
the high window, chin resting
on the cross of his forearms,
gazing into the street
like an overfed watchdog.
Later he would emerge stripped
& walk from room to room,
hairy scrotum swaying like wind chimes,
gathering stacks of loose notes, pamphlets,
periodicals, & drop suddenly to read,
cross-legged, on the carpet.
Towards dawn he would fall asleep
beneath a scavenged sheet on the basement couch,
t.v. on, the alarm set for seven.
Mother said nothing.
And that evening he'd be in the best of moods,
clap me loudly on the back, greet us all
with huge hugs, his sweet, warm breath
short & quick on our necks.

FROM HERE TO L.A.

June already,
the homescreen shook with electric snow,
& in Anaheim
Don Baylor, mired at .174,
swings like a lumberjack in the sodium glare,
his sweaty face carved angular
as a ritual mask.

The midnight air, bloated as a wineskin,
won't even nod toward my windows
propped wide with boards.
A sleek squirrel scratches up
a sprawling maple, & poised on his hind legs
voices a rasping bark, frantic
as a baby's cough.

But now Carew, cool as a white suit
in his relaxed, loosely-coiled stance,
is in the box,
& even the screen, charged snow
gathered in the wings, flicks clear
for this moment.
Dense with concentration,
he bends toward the plate,
meets MacGregor's hard, sliding stuff
& chips a single offside into left
like a man whisking a fly from his dish.

A short, shrill cheer punctuates
the half-filled stands.
Carew, hands on knees,
tap-steps a few feet off first.
From here to L.A., a few of us,
balding, flaccid with heat,
wash our tongues with beer,
our eyes blinking rapidly in applause.

PASADENA

When you hit Pasadena
at 2 A.M., dropped off

by newly-weds in a borrowed van
who had passed once & u-turned
to pluck you, helpless & melting,

from the road at Barstow,
every exposed span of skin
will be windburnt pagoda red,
tender as frog's belly, your steps
stiff as a pharaoh's.

You'll ginger across the strip
toward the shuttered windows of concrete shanties:
in Manhattan your mother
will startle out of her late show daze,
cringe, reach to pull you safe

& grab only velvety, air-conditioned space
while you door-pound the proprietess awake
in her curlers & flannel robe, find yourself
shouting in a whisper that traveller's checks
are better than money,

then falling asleep in your salt-licked t-shirt,
lights on, & thoroughly cooled.

THERE

If you are thumbing West & a trooper in Oklahoma steps from his hog-nosed Plymouth, hands you a yellow warning, tells you you're all right, only half-weird, puts you off US 40, you might begin walking the two-lane stretched long as a blue-note through Vinita, Enid, determined to keep the sun on your back. At first you won't notice—they're lost or on empty—but when someone does stop, you scramble, waving, toward the ark of a red Delta 88 bought in good times, grinning like a Bible salesman, boots loose & clopping on the cinders as you run. The driver is cool-eyed, iron-haired, his mouth webbed with quick lines, & the woman wears a print dress closed by a pin, her hair & freckles the same muted color. They won't ask questions & your backseat companion is glad of it. He carries no I.D., has the wide-awake look of an ex-wino who's maybe seen a ghost, & resembles every fair-haired man who can't be certain whether sod or mud or asphalt will break his next fall. Fair-haired smiles often, half-a-face at a time, watches where he rests his hands, slips around back or into the john at every stop, & somewhere between Barstow & San Berdoo you will notice he has gone for good. But you won't know any of this, nor will it have happened, until you have dreamt it some other time & awaken, the sun level with your eyes, in a backyard along the canal in Venice Beach or under a tree in a park in Westwood, & it will seem days since you have truly rested or been anywhere but there.

BOOTS

I do things that make
so little sense I cannot help
but recognize their folly
even while I am doing them.
Take those boots I wore daily
even as their stitched toplines
worked my calves like paring knives,
my every step dispatching a jolt
up & down my leg like a fishhook,
runnels of blood streaming
toward my ankles like raindrops
converging on a windowpane.
Years of lecturing to my students
about all manner of things
& I still hadn't quite learned
that the contest between shoeleather
& flesh is fixed from the start.
As for those boots, they fit
quite well now, thank you: I have
the scars, like scuffed patches
on an inner tube, to prove it.
They're kept in a foyer closet,
polished, somewhat worn at the heels,
right where I store student papers
I can't find the heart to discard.

Sid Gold was born in Harlem's Sydenham Hospital and raised in various boroughs of New York City. A child of the working class, he has worked on a loading dock, in a scrapyard, as a cabdriver, blueprint trimmer, gas station attendant, housepainter, messenger, customer service representative, legal assistant, and bank teller in addition to a teaching career of twenty-eight years. He studied at SUNY Brockport and the University of Maryland and taught at The George Washington University, Bowie State University, the University of Maryland, and other Washington-area institutions. He lives in Hyattsville, Maryland.

www.ingramcontent.com/pod-product-compliance
Lightning Source LLC
Chambersburg PA
CBHW021511090426
42739CB00007B/553